ROYAL WEDDINGS

Emily Brand

SHIRE PUBLICATIONS

Published in Great Britain in 2011 by Shire Publications Ltd, Midland House, West Way, Botley, Oxford OX2 0PH, United Kingdom.

44-02 23rd Street, Suite 219. Long Island City, NY 11101, USA.

E-mail: shire@shirebooks.co.uk
www.shirebooks.co.uk

A CIP catalogue record for this book is available from the British Library.

Shire Library no. 665.   ISBN-13: 978 0 74781 093 3

Emily Brand has asserted her right under the Copyright, Designs and Patents Act, 1988, to be identified as the author of this book.

Designed by Myriam Bell Design, France and typeset in Perpetua and Gill Sans.
Printed in China through Worldprint Ltd.

11 12 13 14 15   10 9 8 7 6 5 4 3 2 1

COVER IMAGE
The marriage of the Prince of Wales to Princess Alexandra of Denmark at Windsor, 10 March 1863, by William Powell Frith (The Royal Collection © 2010 Her Majesty Queen Elizabeth II).

TITLE PAGE IMAGE
Newlyweds Princess Elizabeth and Prince Philip of Greece on their wedding day, 20 November 1947.

CONTENTS PAGE IMAGE
Ring presented by Prince George, Duke of York (the future George V) to his bride Mary of Teck on 6 July 1893.

ACKNOWLEDGEMENTS
Illustrations are acknowledged as follows:

AKG Images, pages 17, 19 and 20; The Bridgeman Art Library, pages 4 and 14 and 41 (top); British Library Images, pages 10, 12 and 18; Christopher Eimer, pages 9 and 24 (top); Corbis, pages 43, 45, 46, 48 and 50 (top left); Getty Images, title page, page 49 and 52 (top); Heritage Images, page 13 (top); Mary Evans Picture Library, pages 7 (bottom), 13 (bottom), 30, 33 (top), 38, 41 (bottom), 42 and 44; Mirrorpix, pages 51 and 52 (bottom); Museum of London, pages 27, 28, 33 (bottom) and 34; Philip Mould Ltd, London/The Bridgeman Art Library, page 15; The Duke of Norfolk, Arundel Castle/The Bridgeman Art Library, page 7 (top); The Royal Collection © 2010 Her Majesty Queen Elizabeth II, page 29; The Royal Collection/The Bridgeman Art Library, pages 25 and 32; The Stapleton Collection/The Bridgeman Art Library, page 8; Timothy Millett Collection/The Bridgeman Art Library, page 23; Topfoto, page 36 (top); V&A Images, pages 22 (both). Other illustrations are taken from contemporary publications in the possession of the author.

With thanks to Jack, Tom and my parents for all their support, particularly my mother, who never fails to remind me that it's high time I got married myself.

Shire Publications is supporting the Woodland Trust, the UK's leading woodland conservation charity, by funding the dedication of trees.

CONTENTS

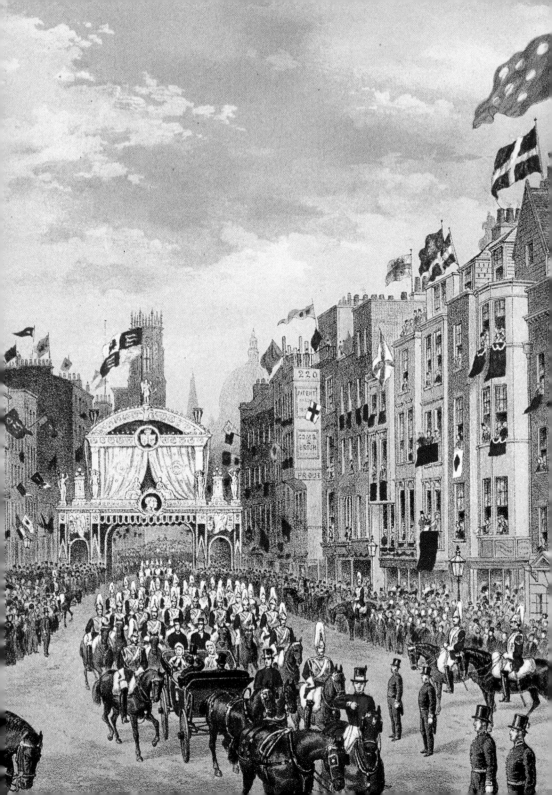

INTRODUCTION

SINCE THE NORMAN CONQUEST, the journey of the oldest and most revered of British institutions, the monarchy, has been touched by turmoil, intrigue, sacrifice and romance. The aims of those taking the throne have varied wildly, and the concept of monarchy itself has been transformed by changing national ideals and international circumstances. But at least one aspect of rule seems to have endured every jolt of the royal carriage. Pomp, pageantry and public ceremony have persisted as central features of the royal court, often at once celebrating and consolidating the power of the monarch at its heart. Stamping the royal seal on significant occasions, from the lavish sporting tournaments of the lost Greenwich Palace to the thirty-eight coronations solemnised within the walls of Westminster Abbey, the history of the British royal family is coloured with self-conscious displays of magnificence.

But what of the most enchanting of all royal occasions, the wedding? In modern times, the mere prospect of such an occasion can stir feverish national and international excitement. Promising a unique blend of stately tradition and contemporary glamour, the marriages of Britain's foremost family have continued to appeal to an increasingly wide audience.

Why should this be? History illustrates that things certainly haven't always been so. Looking back through the centuries, it is clear that both the meaning invested in the royal wedding and the manner in which the ceremonies are conducted have changed dramatically. Venues have varied from the many palaces scattered around London to the sacred grandeur of York Minster and, if we are to believe medieval gossip, a small manor nestled in the woodlands of Northamptonshire. The hurried late-night services that bound some royal couples in matrimony contrast sharply with the splendour and public festivities that attended many others.

Nevertheless, a monarchy whose authority lies in its antiquity cannot be disentangled from the traditions that it inherits. The rituals and symbols springing from allegories of love, political gesture or simply personal preference have become traditions that have been passed down the

Opposite: Crowds line the streets for a glimpse of the procession of Princess Alexandra driving through Temple Bar on her arrival in London, three days before her marriage to the Prince of Wales on 7 March 1863.

5

generations. The European influence, too, is evident — the royal family absorbed the cultural traditions as well as the blood of other nations, and was in turn bound through wedlock into other courts. No doubt owing in part to her own skilful direction and dynastic ambitions, Queen Victoria's impressive brood married into almost every royal house in Europe.

Forging these marital ties with foreign nations was itself something of a routine, even a fixation, for British royalty until the twentieth century. The politics that simmered beneath the request for a hand in matrimony were usually the primary, if not the only, reason for marriage. In fact, the formalities

An example of the illuminated royal wedding decorations adorning Oxford Street in 1893, with the entwined initials of the couple, 'G' and 'M' shining brightly in the middle.

of engagement had most likely already been orchestrated by government officials without a glimmer of concern about the couple's wishes. For the rich in general, and the royal family most particularly, marriage was a mercenary affair of national importance; as writer Hester Chapone lamented in 1773, the whole process took on the aspect of 'mere Smithfield bargains, so much ready money for so much land, and my daughter flung into the bargain!'

The etiquette of a royal wedding might vary according to the status of those entering into wedlock, but wherever possible it was preferred that a foreign bride-to-be should make the journey to be married, and settled, in England. The apprehensions of these young princesses, who had often not yet mastered the language, cannot have been soothed by the fact that they were to become the property of their adoptive nation. A congratulatory sermon composed for the approaching nuptials of Frederick, Prince of Wales and Augusta of Saxe-Gotha in 1736 seems almost ominous in tone:

The wedding ring of Mary of Modena, second wife of James II of England, 1674. The ring is of Italian design, crafted from gold and rubies.

A royal wedding dinner, most probably at the court of Burgundy, in the fifteenth century. A feast would often be followed by dancing and music, sometimes a troupe of singing minstrels accompanied by the harp.

The marriage certificate of the Duke of Kent and Princess Marina of Greece, 29 November 1934. It was at this wedding that the young Princess Elizabeth (later Elizabeth II) first laid eyes on her future husband, Philip Mountbatten.

But thou, O Bride, give Ear,
And to my Words attend;
Forget thy native Country now,
And every former Friend.

The knowledge that her wedding ring would rend her from everything familiar must have occasioned incomparable wedding nerves for the foreign princess accepting the proposal of an English prince. From the Middle Ages to the nineteenth century, the ceremonies themselves were largely private, and unnecessary expense was avoided. If money was to be spent, it was more likely to fund a celebratory feast than a long or lavish service. Unhappily this unsentimental attitude tended to extend to the relationship itself, and few prospective couples laboured under any illusions as to the nature of the matrimonial bond. If they did, their optimism did not last long. It was expected that a man might enjoy his mistresses, being allowed that he might marry for heirs but seek personal satisfaction elsewhere. The notion that emotional commitment within a marriage constitutes a source of strength did not always ring true. In medieval England, kings were often weakened by love.

Despite the careful negotiations preceding a wedding, both public opinion and the highest authorities occasionally expressed their displeasure with the direction royal marriages were taking. The Catholic brides favoured by Stuart kings left a nation of blossoming Protestantism uneasy, and legal restrictions were later introduced in an effort to salvage the royal reputation from a succession of Georgians determined to seek spouses in inappropriate quarters. The unfortunate result was a horde of princes opting to live openly in sin, others going grumbling – or worse, totally inebriated – to the altar, and their spinster sisters sighing for forbidden love in the decaying elegance of Kew Palace. The Victorian era set a refreshing standard of virtuous domesticity for the nineteenth-century family, and the growing public affection for the monarchy cultivated curiosity about life behind the palace doors. The aftermath of the First World War heralded a new era for the British monarchy, and the relaxation of the rules of wedlock introduced the possibility of a royal family prizing genuine love matches over political schemes.

A medallion struck to commemorate the union of Charles I and his French bride Henrietta Maria on 13 June 1625, with images of the royal couple in profile.

Popular festivities had always accompanied the announcement of a royal wedding, although the people of fourteenth-century London were no doubt more excited by the free drink and bonfires than the nuptials of a king they wouldn't even recognise in the street. However, a keener appreciation of stately ceremony was encouraged by a flourishing media culture and a gently softening relationship between crown and country. In recent years, the increasingly public nature of royal ceremony has encouraged the notion of the monarchy as an ordinary family in extraordinary circumstances. In the words of Victorian commentator Walter Bagehot, 'a princely marriage is the brilliant edition of a universal fact, and, as such, it rivets mankind.'

This book charts how the politically charged, private ceremonies that have dominated British history evolved into the often elaborate services we know today. With each wedding drawing from regal tradition and contemporary values, with a spark of modern fashion, the attributes they all share can be comfortably traced, but political maneouvres and religious reforms distinguish some ceremonies markedly from others. The extent to which the public now experiences the royal wedding is perhaps the most striking development of all; in a manner neatly expressed by the American *Life* magazine in 1947, 'In austere Britain, Englishmen gladly finance their monarchy, but in return they demand a good show.'

R . DE . FRANCE .   h . LE . CINQVIESME .

Le premier chapitre de
monstre comment le
roy se en ala a Rainz soy
faire couronner quelque
que emps schrit il leust
En nom
du prix
du filz
du saint
esperit de la glorieuse v.

cirite marie de monseigneur
saint Denis patron de fran
ce et de toute la beatitude ce
leste. cy commencent les
croniques et gestes du temps
de tresscritien roy de fran
ce Charles vij de ce nom fai
tes et compilees par moy
frere Jehan chartier religieu
et chantre de leglise monss

THE NORMANS TO
THE TUDORS

O N CHRISTMAS DAY IN 1066, William the Conqueror became the first
monarch to be crowned in Westminster Abbey, establishing a trend that
has lasted for almost a thousand years. The royal line of the Normans, borne
of violence and conquest, now seemed secure. But throughout the medieval
era, the reigns of his successors resounded with the cries of war and prayers
for a strong heir. England fell in and out of conflict with rising European
powers, each party hungrily seeking to expand its territories. During the
fifteenth century the spirit of war turned inwards, and two royal lines fought
tirelessly in a political see-saw known as the Wars of the Roses. The
culmination of these wars saw the installation of one of the most notorious
dynasties in British history – the Tudors.

At the heart of these grand political events, however, lay the key to
cementing royal power – a bloodline, a family, a wife. The ideal medieval
monarch was a hero on the battlefield and a stallion in the bedchamber, a
model of masculine chivalry to provide his country with strong heirs. The
question of queenship was hotly debated in the sixteenth century, but until
this point women were kept firmly away from reigning alone. Thus, the
most significant royal weddings were a matter of English princes and their
consorts. The ceremonies themselves were fairly routine and did not always
reflect the scale of the politics that underpinned the passion (if there was
any in the first place). Even after the fall of the Lancastrian dynasty, their
guidelines for royal ceremony – laid down in *The Royal Book* – offered a
precedent for their successors. One of the primary concerns was the
decision 'whether the King will be married privily or openly.' The great
majority opted for the former, choosing to stage pageantry instead for their
bride's arrival in the country, or her coronation. In 1540, a member of the
Privy Chamber remarked:

> the State of Princes … in matters of marriage [is] of far worse than the
> condition of poor men. For Princes take as is brought to them by others,
> and poor men be commonly at their own devices and liberty.

Opposite: A retrospective rendering of the marriage of King Henry V of England to Catharine of Valois in 1420, as portrayed in *Chroniques de France ou de Saint Denis* (1487). The wedding took place on French soil, most likely at Troyes Cathedral. The Tudor double rose and the Beaufort portcullis which repeat in the borders advertise the later marriage of Elizabeth of York and Henry VII, which signified a union between the previously warring houses of York and Lancaster.

Opposite top:
The moment
Richard II met his
six-year-old bride,
Isabella of Valois,
from Jean
Froissart's
Chronicles. The
couple were
married on
31 October 1396.

The first of the Norman kings to enter into wedlock on English soil chose to do so in Westminster Abbey. In a move that endeared him to the downtrodden populace, Henry I married Edith, the daughter of a Scottish king, on 11 November 1100. The union did, however, cause unrest among the indignant Norman barons, and in an attempt to assuage their anxieties the queen adopted a more familiar-sounding name, Matilda. The legitimacy of the marriage itself was not untested. Before declaring them married, the Archbishop of Canterbury felt it necessary to inform the crowd that rumours that Matilda was a runaway nun – and therefore already joined with God in matrimony – were unfounded. While the twelfth-century chronicler William of Malmesbury recounts that Henry had 'long been greatly attached' to his bride, her royal parentage certainly presented an undeniable practical asset. Indeed, the extent of his fondness is perhaps suggested by the fact that he subsequently fathered the largest brood of royal bastards in English history. The primary value of the wedding lay in its ability to produce an heir that could reign over both the English and Scottish kingdoms.

In the event, this endeavour was unsuccessful. But its power to solemnise personal alliances and seal treaties between nations elevated the royal marriage to an event of undeniable political weight, centred on the pragmatic choice of bride.

When communications became frosty, a well-calculated foreign match could restore the balance, and for centuries England oscillated between French and Spanish brides depending on the state of European relations. If contending claims to the throne arose, powerful family connections cemented in law could mean the difference between grasping the crown and conceding defeat.

As with the case of Henry 'the Young King' (son of Henry II) and his wife, a couple could be betrothed at a very tender age (here, just five and two years old respectively). In 1172, after an engagement of twelve years, he obediently wed the daughter of the French king in a match orchestrated to benefit the estates of his father. However, it was not exceptional for a king to reconsider his alliances and hastily draw

King Henry I, the first Norman king to marry on English soil.

up a more attractive match in a matter of weeks. Although it was common practice, marrying a near relation also offered a neat opt-out clause. Following his coronation in 1199, King John was so gallant as to drop his first wife, annulling the union on account of a sudden discomfort with their consanguinity, and install a consort who could more readily provide him with children.

Richard II's search for a spouse offers insight into how shifting political moods expressed themselves through marriage, and how willingly a court might relinquish its children to another nation. The vows he took beside Anne of Bohemia forged an alliance against enemy France in the Hundred Years' War. Her death twelve years later set him at liberty to find a new wife, and the king, aged twenty-nine, quickly accepted the six-year-old Isabella of Valois as part of truce negotiations with France. They wed on 31 October 1396. Such an arrangement was not uncommon: to medieval eyes, in less than ten years she would be ready to bear his children.

But in an age of strategic matrimonial alliances, the spirit of romantic love found its royal champion in Edward IV, the first of only two kings to have personally chosen his bride during this era. The secrecy of the affair only added to the romance that rose around it – the king

Below:
An anonymous engraving of King Edward IV. The white rose of York can be seen on his breast.

13

himself did not even admit its existence to his Privy Council for at least five months. Edward first met Elizabeth Woodville, the impoverished widow of a Lancastrian soldier, in 1464; she solicited his help, so it was said, under the boughs of an oak tree. Riding north to meet the enemy forces, the Yorkist king was 'struck by her mournful beauty' and hoped to alleviate her distress by suggesting that she become his mistress. Rebuffed, he whisked her to her father's manor in Grafton to take her as his wife instead. The only people present at the union were Elizabeth's mother, a Dominican priest, a man who 'helped the priest sing', and two anonymous witnesses. Remaining at Grafton for three days, his wife was brought to him secretly each night. He only mentioned this liaison to his councillors when they

Elizabeth Woodville resplendent at her coronation, no doubt in part to atone for her rushed wedding to Edward IV. The pair were married secretly in 1464.

unwittingly drew up plans for a distinctly more profitable foreign match, and the king was roundly condemned for wasting his most powerful political tool. Attempting to atone for the hushed wedding and lend justification to her position as queen consort, a lavish ceremony attended her controversial coronation in 1465.

Edward struggled to prove the credentials of his bride, but a more careful selection of English wife could be instrumental in calming warring domestic factions. As well-connected women played the pawn in political games, a careful match could confer a stronger claim to the English throne. The wedding of Henry VII was perhaps the most prudent of them all, as he finally reconciled the Houses of York and Lancaster by taking the hand of

Left: The only surviving contemporary portrait of Arthur, Prince of Wales. Dated to c. 1499, it was made within a year or two of his marriage to Catherine of Aragon.

Elizabeth of York, simultaneously tightening his own grip on the crown. The rights of their offspring to the succession were impeccable.

With this new stability came the opportunity for public show. The union of their eldest son Prince Arthur to Catherine of Aragon on 14 November 1501 exhibited a blend of grandeur and holiness intended to impress the spectators with the magnificence and divinity of the fledgling Tudor monarchy. In a perfectly orchestrated match, the two had been betrothed since infancy, met after a long correspondence and were married ten days later. Taking their vows at the old St Paul's Cathedral, both bride and groom wore brilliant white. Escorted along the aisle by Arthur's nine-year-old brother Henry, Catherine nervously tottered along a specially assembled platform raised six feet high and draped in red fabric. Before leaving to celebrate the nuptial mass, the newlyweds waved to a crowd estimated at 20,000 spectators.

Arthur's unexpected death just months later brought little Henry in line for the throne, a monarch whose legacy now seems to be defined by his enthusiasm for a royal wedding. Whether or not all of his marriages stand as legitimate (a detail that he himself seemed to reconsider as wives fell from favour), Henry VIII stood as bridegroom six times. He also personally selected four of his six wives from his own court, an indulgence that would not be seen again until the twentieth century.

The contrast between his low-key weddings and that of his elder brother is striking, and all the more so because his first bride was Arthur's widow. While the union sanctified on 11 June 1509 upheld the peace with Spain, reservations about the legitimacy of the union cast a shadow over the occasion. As such, they wed with little ceremony in her apartments at Greenwich Palace. Having failed to produce a male heir, the momentous proceedings by which Henry divorced Catherine of Aragon twenty-four years later plunged England into Protestantism and religious controversy that would last for generations. Accordingly, his marriage to Anne Boleyn was a surreptitious affair. In fact, two services were conducted to ensure its authenticity, the first in Dover and the second at Whitehall 'a little before dawn' on a January morning in 1533. He was most famously displeased with his engagement to Anne of Cleves. Feeling grossly deceived by the portrait he had been shown, he dragged his heels to the altar in Greenwich, grumbling 'if it were not to satisfy the world and my realm, I would not do that I must do this day for none earthly thing.' Seven months later she returned her wedding ring to him, 'desiring that it might be broken in pieces as a thing which she knew of no force or value.' Henry does not seem to have been concerned in distinguishing one ceremony from another. With all taking place at Greenwich or Whitehall Palace, he made the same vows, six times, in a pledge that is familiar even today:

I, Henry, take thee to my wedded wife, to have and to hold from this day forward, for better for worse, for richer for poorer, in sickness and in health, till death us do part, and thereto I plight thee my troth.

At her turn each bride promised the same, before assenting to be 'bonny and buxom in bed and at board.'

Hans Holbein's portrait of Henry VIII in the clothes he wore for his wedding to Anne of Cleves on 6 January 1540.

· ANNO · ÆTATIS ·   · SVÆ · XLIX ·

The nullification document that ended Henry and Anne of Cleves' short-lived marriage just seven months after the ceremony.

Henry's children were less impatient to get to the altar. His successor Edward VI died young and the future Elizabeth I famously declared herself married to her country (consoling herself by meddling in the love-lives of everyone at court instead).

His eldest, and devoutly Catholic, daughter Mary I had introduced the dawn of a 'monstrous regiment of women', according to inflammatory tracts such as that penned by John Knox in 1558. As she assumed the responsibilities of queen regnant, the nation's attitude toward royal marriage toppled into disarray. Proclaiming a strong passion for Philip of

Spain after viewing his Titian portrait, Mary provoked unease in Protestant quarters and those fearing the implications of her promising to obey a foreign husband. She was unmoved, but the lack of popular enthusiasm caused the wedding preparations to fall flat. It took place at Winchester Cathedral just two days after their first meeting, in a ceremony entwined with Spanish Catholic traditions, symbols and courtly fashions.

With the exception of the grand ceremonial of Arthur and Catherine, royal weddings from the eleventh to the sixteenth century remained a predominantly private affair. No matter how deep the national connotations might run, the public could lay no claim to unearthing the intimate details of the marital lives of their monarchs. This was to change, however, as the public concept of the monarchy inched away from divine ordination and the blossoming of print culture provided a welcome instrument for both the politician and the brazen gossip.

The marriage of Queen Mary I to Philip II, King of Spain and Portugal at Winchester Cathedral in 1554, in a painting by Anastasio Fontebuoni (1598).

POPERY AND LAMPOONERY

T HE REIGN of the Stuarts came into being with the death of Elizabeth I, whose refusal to submit to masculine domination earned her respect but denied her an heir. When the crown passed to her Scottish cousin James, it was hoped that the new dynasty might display similar personal strength. But even after the brief republican experiment of the 1650s and the Restoration of the Monarchy in 1660, the matrimonial ventures of the royal family did not always demonstrate so much wisdom as wishful thinking. Many eyebrows were raised by the fact that, while professing their loyalty to the Church of England, Stuart kings persistently pursued Catholic brides. The royal habit of celebrating weddings privately continued unchallenged, at once avoiding prying eyes and unnecessary expenditure. In fact, this practice seems to have been a general trend, and in 1719 it was observed that:

> persons of quality, and many others who imitate them, have lately taken up
> the custom of being marry'd very late at night in their chamber, and often
> at some country house [to] avoid a great deal of expense and trouble.

Nevertheless, snippets of royal news and gossip began to pepper the world of print. Alongside increasing demand for printed accounts of royal weddings, all manner of commemorative medallions and tokens were manufactured, down to the novelty gallery tickets issued by one theatre in 1733. Similarly, gambling dens could prove very lucrative in seventeenth-century England, although the odds were more likely to speculate about the last-minute choice of bride than the wedding date or venue.

In 1625, a detailed account of the marriage of Charles I to the sister of the French king appeared in print. Clearly angling for royal favour, the author proclaims that no blessing could be more glorious than 'this happie and long wisht for Union betweene the two great Monarchies of *France* and *Great Britain*.' This sentiment was by no means universally entertained, and later commentators even held the marriage to account as a principal cause of the Civil War: 'This marriage... was against the main bent and Genius of the

Opposite: A highly idealised rendering of the disastrous wedding of the Prince Regent and Caroline of Brunswick in 1795.

Portrait of Charles and Henrietta Maria, after a portraitof 1632 by Anthony van Dyck to adorn the queen's apartments in Somerset House. The garland of laurel that Henrietta hands over to her husband symbolizes their union, and the olive branch in her other hand perhaps alludes to the peace between the two nations as a result.

Profile portraits of Charles I and Henrietta Maria, set on tokens commemorating their wedding in 1625.

People, and proved one great Occasion of the future Calamities of the Nation.' Although marrying by proxy was not unique, this ceremony was most remarkable for the fact that the lavish service was staged at Notre Dame Cathedral in Paris, and the groom was not even present. Accompanied by an almost warlike fanfare of trumpets, drumming and fifes, the bride Henrietta Maria glittered along the aisle in a golden dress trimmed with diamonds. As she made her vows, she gazed into the eyes of the man representing King Charles, the Duke of Chereuse. Following 'all manner of revells', she journeyed to Dover to finally meet her husband. The couple travelled in state along roads strewn with roses and presented themselves at a feast in the Banqueting House at Whitehall. The Articles of Marriage were read in public and approved by the king, the couple blessed, and 'the King kissed the Queene in presence of the whole people.'

Despite the reputation of the Restoration court for opulence and licentiousness, the wedding of Charles II and Catherine of Braganza on 2 May 1662 was a fairly sober affair. To accommodate both parties two ceremonies were held, one in private by a Roman Catholic priest at their meeting place of Portsmouth, and another conducted by the Bishop of London upon their arrival in the capital. Catherine wore a rose-coloured dress dotted with lovers' knots of blue ribbon, but her choice of attire did not impress – particularly her farthingale, or hooped skirt. Diarist John Evelyn mocked her troupe of 'Portuguese ladies into their monstrous farthingales', adding, 'Her Majesty had the same habit, her foretop long and turned aside very strangely.' It seems that the poor bride was unaware that this style of dress had been unfashionable in England for decades. Charles's own view of the proceedings is perhaps evocative of the spirit of the occasion: 'I was happy the honour of the nation that I was not put to the consummation of the marriage last night … as I was afraid that matters would have gone very sleepily.'

In their turn, his nieces Mary and Anne submitted quietly to the matches made for them, the former no doubt cringing as her uncle winked and led the couple to the bed, bellowing 'to your work, nephew!' English princesses were not exempt from the marital negotiations that could herald their removal to another country and culture. One October evening in 1677, Mary's father took her by the hand and informed her that she was to wed William, Prince of Orange. Leaving her in tears, which persisted for two days, he made the happy announcement to the Privy Council. On 4 November, the wedding party assembled in Mary's bedchamber for the service. It was 'announced with great pomp' from London to

Edinburgh, where arbours of the Prince's fruit transformed the town centre into a vision of orange, 'great bonfires were kindled [and] the popular rejoicings were prolonged till a late hour.' Although they departed for Holland a week later, they returned in 1689 to be crowned as the only joint monarchs in English history. Despite her misgivings, their relationship was happy, but they were unable to have children.

Her sister Anne's tragic inability to provide the nation with a living heir, having suffered the loss of as many as eighteen children to miscarriage and infant mortality, introduced the House of Hanover to the throne. Chosen for his unimpeachable Protestantism, George I took the crown seven years after the union with Scotland and was proclaimed King of Great Britain in 1714. His heirs were to rule on the condition that they abided by legislation passed in 1689 and 1701 that barred Roman Catholics and their spouses from ascending the throne. While these parliamentary decrees effectively ended the religious anxieties that had so long clouded royal marriages, England was hard pressed to get too excited about the wives the Georgians chose. Openly reluctant to embrace the nation as their own, or even to learn the language, the first two Georgian kings pined for their German homeland. The children of George II were the first Hanoverian royals to celebrate their nuptials on English soil, but the matches were clearly devised by their father. On 4 May 1736, the *Dublin Post* reported its joy that the king had 'strengthened the Protestant interest, by bestowing his eldest daughter on the Prince of Orange'

This detail from a commemorative medallion portrays the marriage of Mary Henrietta Stuart, the Princess Royal, and William II of Orange. They wed in the Chapel Royal of Whitehall Palace on 2 May 1640. Their only son, William III, would go on to become joint monarch of England with his wife Mary in 1689.

and 'completed our security' by forcing the Prince of Wales to renounce his mistresses and furnishing him with a partner to 'warm the Hearts of Protestants and Englishmen.' These two weddings, in 1733 and 1736 respectively, offered the court a chance to flaunt their finery. In the weeks preceding Prince Frederick's union with Augusta of Saxe-Gotha, *The Old Whig* noted that even the queen's birthday celebrations were somewhat muted, 'the Nobility reserving themselves to appear with greater Lustre at his Royal Highness's Wedding.' Those on the fringes of courtly circles felt less impressed, as one female observer sighed to a friend: 'monstrous preparations are making for the royal wedding… I am too poor and too dull to make one among the fine multitudes.' Clearly, royal weddings were being subjected to a new kind of public scrutiny.

This medallion portrays Augusta, Princess of Wales, the slightly queasy bride of Prince Frederick, and mother of George III. It was struck to commemorate her death in 1772.

Prince Frederick wed Augusta in the Chapel Royal of St James's Palace, three years after his sister. Although Hans Holbein had originally ornamented the room in honour of Henry VIII's ill-fated union with Anne of Cleves, an undaunted flock of royals married here throughout the eighteenth and nineteenth centuries. In 1736, the crowds gathered outside and the service ran smoothly, although some sources reported that the teenage bride was so nervous that she vomited onto the queen's skirt. Frederick's premature death meant that the pair never took the throne, but the privilege passed directly to their eldest son George in 1760. He was proclaimed sovereign, married and crowned amidst a whirl of pageantry in the space of a year.

As the writer and lexicographer Samuel Johnson postulated at the time, 'a show without spectators cannot be a show.' In an age of blossoming national spirit, it followed that a king without the support of his public could no longer lay claim to leading a true monarchy. Although he may have been something

King George III dons military attire in this print of 1821, produced in the year following his death.

of an awkward, stammering youth, George III certainly recognised this. Immediately impressing the nation with the declaration 'Born and educated in this country, I glory in the name of Britain', he dutifully married the best of an unattractive troupe of eligible German princesses, Charlotte of Mecklenburg-Strelitz. Furthermore, in an almost unheard-of instance of matrimonial loyalty, he didn't take a mistress for the entirety of their marriage.

As the wedding date approached, one journalist bemoaned:

> the present complection of the people is such, that I find it absolutely vain
> and ridiculous to attempt writing to them on any other subject than that of
> the Royal Wedding and Coronation … Scarce a paragraph of news, relating
> to any other matters, will go down.

The alehouses of London took the opportunity to advertise their finest new
'Mecklenburg purl and Coronation porter' and courtiers rushed to purchase
commemorative fans and fashion accessories for the occasion. After the
ceremony on 8 September, Horace Walpole was characteristically critical of
the bride's dress:

> The Queen was in white and silver, and an endless mantle of violet covered
> velvet, lined with ermine, and attempted to be fastened on her shoulder by
> a bunch of large pearls, dragged itself and almost the rest of her clothes
> halfway down her waist.

The effect of this disastrous choice, he continued, was that the guests now
knew as much of the upper half of the queen as the king himself!

George III with
wife Queen
Charlotte and their
six eldest children,
painted by Johann
Zoffany in 1770.
Despite tentative
beginnings, their
marriage was
certainly fruitful
and Charlotte
provided George
with fifteen
children,
thirteen of whom
survived to
adulthood. They
were to be no
more prudent
than the king's
troublesome
siblings in
matrimonial
matters, much
to his dismay.

It was during the later eighteenth century that the notion of marrying for love began to glimmer as a national ideal, but the social circles that resisted this most strongly were the aristocracy, and most pointedly, royalty. In 1772, the Royal Marriages Act underlined the king's frustration with the disreputable matches his unruly siblings seemed determined to pursue. Perhaps harbouring a touch of resentment that he had fulfilled *his* matrimonial duty, he decreed that his immediate relations could not enter into wedlock without his permission, or that of parliament. Despite his best efforts the king faced worse from his own brood, most famously from his heir George, Prince of Wales (later George IV). The prince's clandestine union with the Catholic Maria Fitzherbert in 1785 was declared null and void, and his furious father demanded that he contract a more propitious marriage. Renowned as a young rake inclined to 'drink, wench and swear like a man who at all times would prefer a girl and a bottle to politics and a sermon', he was only persuaded by parliament's promise to clear his enormous debts if he obeyed.

His subsequent relationship with Caroline of Brunswick is one of the most famously turbulent of all English royal matches, and even the wedding service presaged the hostility to come. Unimpressed by the 'bouncing, romping princess' presented to him, George's initial reaction was to splutter 'Harris, I am not well; pray get me a glass of brandy.' Unable to recollect his marital obligations as stoically as his father, he derided her lack of hygiene and flaunted his buxom mistresses before her at every opportunity. For her part, Caroline loudly expressed her disappointment that he was less attractive than his portrait.

The preparations marched onwards. The Chapel Royal at St James's was adorned with crimson and gold, and extra galleries were added for 'a Band

Bottom left: Contemporary print of George IV in his later years, during the protracted and ultimately unsuccessful struggle to divorce Caroline.

Bottom right: Caroline is also thought to have embarked on a string of affairs and, to her husband's joy, spent most of her time living in Italy between 1814 and 1820.

An interior view of the Crimson Drawing room of Carlton House, as it was ornamented for the marriage of Princess Charlotte and Prince Leopold in 1816.

of Vocal and Instrumental Performers', who played the wedding anthem that had been composed by Handel for his late grandfather's marriage. The efforts only served to highlight the disaster that was the ceremony, which took place on 8 April 1795. The prince reeled into the chapel 'quite drunk', and stumbled up the aisle supported by the Dukes of Bedford and Roxborough. At one point appearing to attempt an escape, he mumbled his vows and barely stifled his sobs when nobody objected to the proceedings. He spent most of his wedding night unconscious in the grate at the opposite side of the room to his wife. By all accounts the nuptial bed was abandoned as soon as possible, but nine months later Caroline bore their only child, Charlotte.

Although the young Princess Charlotte exhibited the makings of a rather spoiled child, in the wake of her debaucherous uncles and distinctly boring spinster aunts, she was a sparkling diamond in the rough. Her engagement to the German Prince Leopold heralded the coming of a younger, mutually affectionate royal family. The ceremony took place on 2 May 1816 at her father's residence Carlton House, beautifully bedecked in crimson velvet and gold.

Her dress was described at great length in fashion periodicals, with *The Lady's Magazine* in raptures over the wreath of roses in her hair, and a gown 'composed of a most magnificent silver lama on net ... fastened in front with a most brilliant and costly ornament of diamonds.' It seems, however, that her deportment may have left something to be desired, as one guest wrote in puzzlement that 'she had not the least gentility of appearance and her manners were shockingly vulgar.' He somewhat undermines the romance of the occasion by adding 'she took very little notice of the service and seemed, from her uneasiness, to wish that it were ended.' She must have been listening, however, because she giggled audibly as the disadvantaged groom promised, 'with all my worldly goods I thee endow.'

Her death in childbirth the following year was universally lamented as a family tragedy and national crisis; with her demise, the king had over fifty grandchildren, and not a legitimate heir among them. The prospect of securing the throne initiated a desperate royal scramble to the altar, as her father's siblings abandoned their mistresses and hurriedly proposed to eligible princesses half their age. If a silver lining was required, the princes found it in the form of a hefty allowance from the government when they entered into wedlock. As a result, the year 1818 saw four royal weddings in as many months. In a match she had been pursuing for years, the Princess Elizabeth finally netted the Prince of Hesse-Hombourg at Buckingham House (later Palace). The choice was unpopular, with his unfashionable moustache and inclination for pipe-smoking apparently offending English sensibilities. His nickname 'humbug' quickly extended to the rest of the royals clamouring to climb into the nuptial bed, and 'humbugging' became a favourite topic of the satirists poking fun at what they saw as the politically inspired nymphomania of the whole family.

The summer months saw three royal brothers each take a German wife. After each union was solemnised in the bride's homeland, second ceremonies were held in London; first for the Duke of Cambridge and Augusta of Hesse at

An engraving of Princess Charlotte and her new husband on their wedding day. The print was published in *La Belle Assemblée* in June 1816.

Buckingham House, and next a remarkable double ceremony at Kew Palace on 11 July. This service would secure the nation's future. In 1830 the Duke of Clarence and his bride would be pronounced Queen Adelaide and King William IV. Following the death of the latter, it would be the only child of Prince Edward, Duke of Kent, and his wife Victoria who would take the crown. Popular enthusiasm for these occasions was notably subdued. Perhaps the novelty was simply too worn, or perhaps the public was tired with subsidising a family for which it held little affection. A flurry of satirical prints represented the financial grants the royals received as a contemptible drain on the pockets of the nation.

The Georgian taste for celebrity and scandal had intensified popular interest in the monarchy, and there were clearly new rules by which it had to abide if it wanted to enjoy public support. In an era drawing increasing attention to the poverty of the masses, it was deemed prudent to keep the patently mercenary marriages as private as possible. However, the new standards of nuptial harmony and royal domesticity ushered in with the Victorian era were to sow the seeds of a more open approach to celebrating royal occasions.

The wedding dress Charlotte wore was met with universal admiration, even if her deportment was somewhat lacking in grace. *The Lady's Magazine* gushed: 'The whole dress surpassed all conception in the brilliancy and richness of its effects.'

THE NINETEENTH CENTURY

IN OCTOBER 1839, the twenty-year-old Queen Victoria proposed to Prince Albert of Saxe-Coburg, as was proper for a couple of their respective stations. The initial distaste she had expressed for arranged marriages dissolved when she saw him, and after their engagement she scribbled in her journal 'he is perfection in every way — in beauty, in everything!' Perhaps the most striking aspect of the union was how much control Victoria exerted in every detail, from formalising the engagement to selecting the materials for her dress. As the plans advanced amid a whirl of popular excitement, she wrote in her diary: 'talked of wearing my robes at the wedding, which I wished not.' Instead, she opted for a white silk and satin dress that was to set a pattern for the rest of the century. The court train was embellished with a tumbling border of orange blossom embroidery, a traditional symbol of betrothal and affection. While floral motifs were always popular in bridal fashion, the custom for wearing this flower had just begun to supersede the tradition for wearing roses, as her cousin Charlotte had. Electing a dress of Honiton lace and Spitalfields silk, the young queen was intentionally supporting local manufacturers, but she proudly adorned herself with the elegant jewelled gifts that Albert had presented to her as tokens of his affection. The groom himself wore the uniform of a British Field Marshal.

St James's Palace again played host to the ceremony, as it would for many of her children, even though Victoria thought the resident choir sang 'schockingly'; the regality of the location clearly atoned for any lack of musical proficiency. In a significant departure from the matrimonial practices of her ancestors, it was decreed that the ceremony would take place at noon, allowing for a full day of festivity. The morning weather was inclement, and the crowds lining the procession route from Buckingham Palace to St James's fought to withstand the 'torrents of rain, and violent gusts of wind.' The queen's spirits were not dampened, however, and she sent her husband-to-be an excited note as soon as she awoke: 'Dearest, how are you today and have you slept well? What weather!' The queen entered the chapel to a flourish of

Opposite: A late nineteenth-century print from *The Illustrated London News* gives an overview of the highly idealised domestic life of the royal family. Small inset portraits of Queen Victoria and Prince Albert and their nine children surround images of their wedding day in 1840, and their young family.

31

silver trumpets, the procession led by the Prime Minister Lord Melbourne (who was 'built like a seventy-four gun ship' according to one observer) and followed by a flock of bridesmaids. The service ran smoothly, lasting only fifteen minutes or so. The roaring thunder of the guns signalled to the crowds that the vows had been exchanged, and the royal procession made its way back to Buckingham Palace for the wedding breakfast.

Perhaps because of the success of her own wedding, or perhaps because it simply would not do to allow the young to arrange their own ceremonies, Victoria insisted on being consulted on royal matches, both of her children and her grandchildren in their turn. The relationship between Albert and Victoria continued in respect and love, and as the 1850s progressed they

Franz Xavier Winterhalter's portrait of Queen Victoria in her wedding attire, including the sapphire brooch Albert had given her the the evening before the ceremony. The painting was commissioned for the couple's seventh wedding anniversary.

began to look forward to the expected flurry of royal weddings as their own children came of age.

It began with the Princess Royal's engagement to Frederick William of Prussia, contrived when she was just 14. Although it was not publicly announced for two years, it suited such a convenient purpose against the threat of Russian growth in Europe that popular speculation had long attached the two. The only negativity in the press came from insinuations that he simply wasn't good enough for their princess (coming from a 'paltry German dynasty' according to *The Times*), but such grumblings softened as it seemed that the couple were genuinely attached, and he was soon 'beloved Fritz'. Before long 'the cheapest popular publication

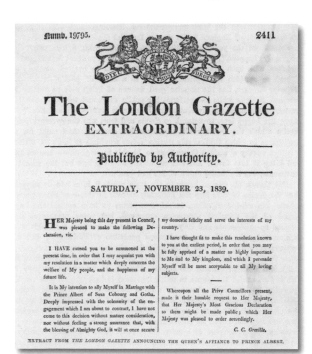

The young Queen Victoria's public announcement of her marriage was widely printed, including this extract from the *London Gazette* on 23 November 1839.

and the humblest shop-window gave evidence of the general goodwill.' When the suggestion came from Prussia that the ceremony should take place in the groom's homeland, Queen Victoria was left 'speechless with indignation.' The royal foot being firmly put down, she retorted, 'whatever may be the usual practice of Prussian Princes, it is not *every* day that one marries the eldest daughter of the Queen of England.'

Instead, the couple entered into wedlock in the same chapel as her parents on the bitterly cold morning of 25 January, 1858. Declared an 'English holyday', the chill did little to discourage 'the million of people or thereabouts who were on their legs … seeking enjoyment from the spectacle of the PRINCESS ROYAL'S wedding'. According to a reporter for *The Times*, the crowds 'cheered lustily' as the procession was being prepared, 'sometimes probably giving a vociferous welcome to a highly adorned underling of the Palace, under the impression that he was some great

Right: This finger ring commemorates the nuptials of Queen Victoria and Prince Albert. Six dozen of these rings were ordered and presented to friends and relations of the royal couple at the time of their marriage in 1840. The ring is made of gold, rimmed with blue enamel, inset with forget-me-not turquoises, diamonds and two miniature medals of Victoria and Albert.

personage.' Of course, although the public was entertained with festivities and illuminations, they were not granted admittance to the ceremony itself. Described as 'pretty and lighthearted', perhaps the most notable aspect of the service was its role in popularising Felix Mendelssohn's comparatively little-known musical suite 'Opus 61', now known as the 'Wedding March'.

The death of Prince Albert in 1862 occasioned the postponement of their second daughter Alice's wedding, and cast a gloom over the queen from which she would never recover. So as not to offend her mourning mother, when Princess Alice finally married Louis of Hesse in July the ceremony was kept low-key, and solemnised in a manner 'as private as possible'. Set for March the following year, the wedding of the future Edward VII to Alexandra of Denmark remained largely under the control of the queen. She bemoaned the excited chatter of her eldest daughter, sighing, 'Dear child! Your ecstasy at the whole thing is to me very incomprehensible.' However, the younger Victoria's spirits were not to be suppressed, not least because of the elegance that the new princess promised to inject back into the sombre court: 'Her voice, her walk, carriage and manner are perfect, she is one of the most ladylike and aristocratic looking people I ever saw!'

Menu card for the Royal Wedding Breakfast in 1893, adorned with the floral symbols that often attend royal marriages, including the roses, thistles and shamrocks representing the components of Great Britain, and the white rose befitting the new Duke and Duchess of York.

THE
ROYAL WEDDING BREAKFAST.
THURSDAY, 6TH JULY, 1893.

POTAGES.
Bernoise à l'Impératrice.
Crème de Riz à la Polonaise.
ENTRÉES (CHAUDES).
Côtelettes d'Agneau à l'Italienne.
Aiguillettes de Canetons aux Pois.
RELEVÉS.
Filets de Bœuf à la Napolitaine.
Poulets Gras au Cresson.
ENTRÉES (FROIDES).
Chauds Froids de Volaille aux Légumes.
Salades de Homard et Saumon.
Galantines de Volaille à l'Aspic.
Filets de Veau à la Gelée.

Haricots Verts.   Epinards.

Kälte Schaale von Früchten.
Pâtisserie assortie.

SIDE TABLE.
Cold Fowl.   Cold Beef.
Tongue.

Apparently determined that the nation was not yet ready for unadulterated festivity, the queen controversially ordered that the location for the wedding should be Windsor Castle, which had not seen a royal wedding since the fourteenth century. This caused a flutter of apprehension among the press, who expected the union of their future monarchs to be a more accessible affair, and not, as *Punch* sardonically remarked, in 'an obscure Berkshire village, noted only for an old castle with bad drains.' Dress codes of half-mourning were still a prerequisite for guests, turning the company into a cloud of lilac, white and grey. The queen herself wore black and observed the proceedings from a private box above the crowd. Happily the bride was exempt from the sartorial restrictions, wearing a fashionable white satin court gown 'trimmed with chatelaines of orange blossom, myrtle and bouffantes of tulle Honiton lace'. According to a German custom signifying affection and hopes for good fortune, the myrtle in her bouquet was

grown from a sprig carried in the bouquet of the Princess Royal in 1858. The service was lengthy and the bride's nerves were betrayed by her 'crimson flush' and whispered vows. According to one souvenir publication, even the Queen's band seemed 'overwrought' - when the guns thundered outside, they hurriedly began tuning their instruments before the Archbishop had even concluded the service.

The next ceremony of national importance was that of their son George, Duke of York, to his bride Princess Mary of Teck, in July 1893. Mary had originally been intended for his elder brother Albert, until his death just a month before they were due to be married. Public sympathy for the grieving 'Princess May' and the gentle duke thrown into the line of succession quickly blossomed into joy at their engagement. After consultation with his grandmother, St James's Palace was adorned with red and white flowers gathered from the royal gardens in preparation for the nuptials. After a string of weddings openly taking the opportunity to boost money for native manufacturers, the royal couple found that suppliers were falling over themselves to offer their services. Lacemakers from Devon provided lace leaf in a cherub design for royal fans, and rivals from Amersham made silver lace to trim the bridesmaids' dresses.

The bride seemed overwhelmed, exclaiming 'we get trousseau things sent to us from all parts of England, Scotland and Ireland so that we are nearly

The Duke of York and his bride, with the bridesmaids, from *The Illustrated London News*, 15 July 1893.

Above: Princess Mary of Teck's wedding dress, 1893.

driven mad and have not a moment's peace.' In the event, her dress was considered a triumph, described by *The Illustrated London News* as 'a white and silver brocade with a pattern of clustered roses, thistles and shamrocks' and trails of orange-blossom, in a design 'typical of Britain and Ireland.' After Mary reached the altar, to the strains of the Bridal March from Wagner's *Lohengrin*, the service began with a choir singing a hymn composed in honour of the occasion. Outside, a vast throng of spectators enjoyed the atmosphere and waited for the royal party to appear. A gossip columnist for *The Sketch* wrote:

I mixed on wedding day with the unwashed in St James's Park. Heavens! Extreme merriment was caused when a seedy man, under the influence of ginger beer and the sun probably, sat down in the middle of the cleared roadway, and declined to move until four policemen united their persuasions.

Right: The wedding breakfast-room at Buckingham Palace on the morning of the marriage of George, Duke of York and Princess Mary of Teck.

After the procession to sign the register at Buckingham Palace, the queen encouraged the newlyweds to make an appearance on the front balcony, before a delighted crowd. Apparently pleased with the adoring scenes below, chairs were ordered and the party sat there for ten minutes. At the wedding breakfast, the contented royal grandmother toasted the couple and commented, no doubt with a hint of self-congratulation, 'it has all been very prettily arranged.'

The British royals of the nineteenth century suffered their share of sorrows, but enjoyed more public affection than many of their ancestors. Warmth towards Buckingham Palace resulted from the popular opinion that 'Her Majesty has reigned gently and prudently … and the Royal Family has set an admirable example of domestic life.' While the nation may have occasionally grumbled that they expected more of a show, they appreciated that at the heart of the ceremonies was a sense of familial duty and devotion.

However, the empire that gave the political nation such comfort was about to be rocked by war and revolution that swept away many of the crowned dynasties of Europe. The British monarchy emerging from the ravages of the First World War wore a very different countenance, and the public was invited to take a more active role in royal ceremony. The royal house would, once and for all, throw off the 'cold glamour of thrones.'

Above, left: The new Duchess of York bends to receive congratulations from the elderly Queen Victoria after the wedding ceremony, 1893. The queen had been instrumental in ensuring that the day ran smoothly.

Above right: The royal couple's stunning wedding cake, made by the queen's baker at Windsor castle.

THE 'DEMOCRATIC' WEDDING

KING GEORGE V AND QUEEN MARY were crowned in the summer of 1911. The conflict and austerity that were to blight the early years of his reign were at least allayed by the mood of solidarity and national pride of the British war effort. As the prospect of peace peeped over the horizon, the image of the monarchy was irrevocably changed and the king was keen to dispense with the German roots and traditions of the British royal house. In 1917, the family name Saxe-Coburg-Gotha was abandoned in favour of Windsor, German titles were abandoned, and the marriage customs by which the royal family had been restrained for so long were relaxed. Pivotally, the tendency to choose a German spouse would no longer be favoured over a match with an honest, loyal British subject. One contemporary newspaper bellowed, 'throughout the Empire the decision to avoid the German taint has been received with approval', and George noted in his diary, 'it was an historic day.' Seeming to throw off the shackles of matrimonial politics, the new generation of royal weddings became hopelessly veiled in the romance and optimism of a kingdom recovering from the horrors of war. On the announcement of the engagement of Princess Mary and Viscount Lascelles, the *Daily Mail* gushed: 'the charm of the match is it leaves no taste of scheming dynastic politics. It is just an English girl and an Englishman who have fallen in love.' The fairytale wedding was coming into full bloom, and it became a distinctly more 'democratic' occasion with the rise of new modes of communication and international media.

The ceremonies held for the marriages of Princess Patricia of Connaught and Princess Mary, in 1919 and 1922 respectively, both took place in Westminster Abbey, allowing for a considerably larger guest list. While it had long been conventional for the groom to wear military uniform, the custom had acquired new connotations in recent years and wearing full armed services dress became a much more general practice for many male wedding guests. The ceremonies of this new era were met with pleasure because they seemed to evoke all of the values the nation now held closer to their hearts,

Opposite: Prince Albert, Duke of York (later King George VI) poses with bride Lady Elizabeth Bowes-Lyon (later Queen Elizabeth, the Queen Mother) on 26 April 1923. The couple were held in great popular esteem, but never expected to become heirs to the throne.

Above: A *Punch*
cartoon of 1917
entitled 'A Good
Riddance', depicting
King George V
sweeping away the
German titles and
traditions that had
been an integral
part of the British
monarchy for
generations.

Right: The wedding
party assembled
for the union of
Princess Mary and
Viscount Lascelles
on 28 February
1922. Along with
the earlier
marriage of
Princess Patricia of
Connaught, they
were setting the
new trend for
taking their vows
at Westminster
Abbey.

and were made, as one American periodical observed, 'in the best British tradition: calm, solemn and humble before God.'

The wedding of the king's second son, Albert, to Elizabeth Bowes-Lyon, daughter of the Earl of Strathmore, illustrates that even those not intended for the throne could stir great excitement. Gratifying the public's renewed taste for glamour and curiosity about radical new fashions, the press finally offered a glimpse of what went on behind the closed doors of the royal house. Gleefully scrutinising and applauding the wedding plans (most crucially, of course, the dress), illustrated magazines sold in droves. The Duke became the first royal groom to marry in the uniform of the newest branch of the armed forces, the Royal Air Force, following his training at Cranwell. The ivory chiffon and lace bridal gown, described by *The Times* as 'the simplest ever made for a royal wedding', embraced an overtly contemporary style but did not forsake the traditional elegance fitting for a new duchess. The veil she wore – lent by Queen Mary – was secured by myrtle leaves, the floral symbol of love and constancy that had ornamented every royal bridal ensemble since Queen Victoria. Continuing the new vogue for a Westminster service, the wedding was set for 26 April 1923. Elizabeth herself established a tradition during this ceremony which has lasted to this day. Honouring the sacrifices of those lost during the Great War, including her

elder brother, she placed her bouquet on the Tomb of the Unknown Warrior on her way to the altar. This touching display of humility and grace on the part of the bride was a subtle but powerful symbol that everyone's perceptions of English society and its monarchy had changed.

Making the procession from the Abbey in the Glass Coach, the couple passed a sea of fluttering handkerchiefs and raised hats, and waved at the crowds enduring the splatters of morning rain. Their carriage departed for the honeymoon amid a shower of rose petals. By the evening, silent motion pictures of the processions to and from the Abbey were available for public viewing nationwide. Indicating the strength of national interest, the headline for the *New York Times* the following day read, with more than a touch of romance: 'Duke of York weds simple Scotch Maid – Little bride appears overwhelmed.' As they settled into married life, the *Pathé Gazette* ran a

Above: The wedding dress worn by Mary, eldest daughter of George V at her wedding to Viscount Lascelles.

special feature on the home life of the new Duke and Duchess of York, allowing the public to further explore the nuances and practical aspects of royal domesticity, from their relationship to their choices of interior design.

Left: Lady Elizabeth Bowes-Lyon in her wedding dress outside her parents' house in Bruton Street, London, as she departs for Westminster Abbey to take her vows.

41

Fashions and Fancies.

Everything for the Bride. It would be almost impossible to keep one's thoughts from straying to the absorbing subject of bridal array this week, and the sketches on this page are offered as a suggestion to those who are soon to follow the royal example. Silver lace and silver embroidery play an important part in many fashionable wedding gowns, and the lovely dress shown here is of white charmeuse, decorated in this way. Victorian, Egyptian, and strictly modern styles share the honours where bridal gowns are concerned this spring, and a departure from the conventional complete white

The simpler the arrangement of the veil, the greater the charm.

toilette is the new idea of using only gold tissue and gold lace. Certainly the all-gold bride looks very effective, and throws the bridegroom even more into the shade than usual !

Bouquet-Making as an Art. Small children are undoubtedly the most ornamental attendants for the bride, and one of the only drawbacks is that they have such an unfortunate knack of either dropping their bouquets altogether at the wrong moment, or, at any rate, of letting slip some of the flowers. Practical fashion

An idea for small bridesmaids: flower-filled baskets of white wistaria wood.

has surmounted the difficulty by introducing the bridesmaid's basket, which tiny folk can manage far more easily than a bouquet. Goodyear, of the Royal Arcade, Old Bond Street, is the artist in flower arrangement who is responsible for the lovely bride's bouquet. Those exquisite Mollie Charman Crawford roses are used, and with them are lilies of the valley, while on the long tulle streamers which hold the flowers are scattered, as though by a careless hand, stray lily-of-the-valley sprays.

Real Butterflies. The latest idea in connection with bouquets is to mount real English butterflies on the flowers they actually visit. This wonderful florist would never dream of posing them on tulips or bluebells, for these flowers are not in bloom in the butterfly season. Bridesmaids' favours are coming into their own again, and so are the old-fashioned bouquets which were once an indispensable part of a coachman's livery. Court bouquets can be had from 17s. 6d. each.

The Wedding Cake. The general verdict on the beautiful wedding cake prepared by McVitie

A lovely bridal gown of white charmeuse and silver lace.

and Price for the marriage of Princess Mary and Viscount Lascelles was that it was far too perfect a piece of workmanship to submit to the indignity of being eaten. The same applies to the really wonderful cake that these world-famous biscuit-manufacturers have contributed to the event of the week. It is well worthy of its prestige, and stands 9 ft. in height, yet, in spite of its weight, which is approximately 800 lb., it is almost fairy-like in the delicacy of its construction. Tier after tier, each decorated in a different manner, rise upwards in a long, tapering design to the summit, where little cupids stand distributing flowers. The bowl itself is of repoussé work, showing the new combined

A profusion of roses and lilies of the valley. Sprays of the latter are scattered over the tulle streamers.

coat of arms, and it holds a magnificent bouquet of roses, lilies of the valley, and white orchids tipped with mauve. Sugar lace is the chief feature of the decoration.   E. A. R.

Brocade shoes for the bride.

One of countless bridal fashion features inspired by the prospect of a wedding. This column looks at contemporary trends amid celebrations for the royal marriage of 1923, and features a veil and gown similar to that worn by Elizabeth Bowes-Lyon.

The country was holding its breath in its anticipation for Albert's elder brother Edward to take a wife. When he ascended the throne in 1936, he threw the government into disarray with his swift proposal to twice-divorced American socialite, Wallis Simpson. The union, which would contradict Edward's monarchical role as Supreme Governor of the Church of England, also caused unease because it was feared that the public would never welcome her as queen. Clearly, despite the fervour for true-love matches, royal suitors were still required to fall in love with someone appropriate. The matter closed with the king's abdication and a discreet wedding at a French château. The newly titled Duke and Duchess of Windsor were to hold little to no authority in stately matters. After thirteen years of enchanting the nation with their comparatively mild-mannered *mode de vie*, Albert and his wife succeeded to the throne as King George VI and Queen Elizabeth.

It was not long before international conflict again brought Britain into the grip of austerity, but the royal family's refusal to be ruffled by the German threat inspired respect and hope in their subjects. As the nation emerged from war and their eldest daughter Elizabeth turned her thoughts to marriage, it might be reasonable to assume that the country would have been unwilling to entertain the idea of an elaborate and expensive ceremony.

Although some such grumblings may have surfaced on occasion, a glamour-starved public had leapt with alacrity onto the weddings of her aunts two decades earlier, and even more eagerly to that of Elizabeth and Lieutenant Philip Mountbatten in 1947.

The couple had first met in 1934, at the wedding of her uncle, the Duke of Kent, to Philip's cousin, Princess Marina of Greece. Their own engagement was officially announced on 9 July 1947, and preparations were made for the ceremony on 20 November. Although no national holiday was declared, the public's desire to be involved was obvious as Britain was deluged with such a massive range of commemorative items that the authorities made efforts to restrain their manufacture.

The invitation list saw the world's royalty descend upon London, and for the first time the procession was broadcast live on television, followed by a full report on the BBC the next morning. The radio, having secured a wide audience during wartime, allowed for reports of the ceremony to be broadcast around the world in forty-two languages. The media coverage eclipsed anything the country had seen before and the streets of London buzzed with excited spectators, some of whom had taken up their positions the previous day, 'equipped with blankets and pillows, camp stools and air mattresses.' One reporter explained this popular enthusiasm with the statement, 'the wedding was a family wedding for the entire British people.'

As ever, at the centre of attention was the bridal dress, for which she had famously saved up ration cards. Created by prominent fashion designer Norman Hartnell, it was described as both 'romantic and regal', and reputedly took its inspiration from Botticelli's *Primavera*, featuring Flora, the classical goddess of spring. The train was 15 feet long, scattered with a floral design incorporating the white rose of York and ears of wheat, a symbol of fertility. Around the neckline gently rested garlands of pearl and orange blossom, with a touch of diamante. As she walked along the aisle, her train was carried

The Duke and Duchess of Windsor after their marriage at the Chateau de Cande in Monts, France, on 8 June 1937. The former King Edward VIII became the only British king in history to abdicate the throne in order to marry according to his own wishes.

The front cover of *The Illustrated London News Royal Wedding Number* celebrates the nuptials of the heir apparent and her new husband. Miniatures of the two nestle among flowers and wedding bells, above Westminster Abbey.

by two young pageboys wearing kilts of Royal Stuart tartan and frilled white shirts. Although she had chosen not to wear the heavy heirloom lace normally bequeathed to a young royal bride, the entire ensemble was coloured with the traditional symbols and imagery of British royal history, from the Wars of the Roses to the Stuarts and the Victorians.

Officiated by the Archbishop of Canterbury, the wedding service followed the normal order of the Church of England. The wedding procession began to make its way out of the Abbey after almost an hour, but not before the newlyweds, hand in hand, paused to curtsey and bow to the bride's grandmother Queen Mary. In a tradition initiated at Mary's own marriage, after the wedding breakfast the newlyweds appeared to wave to the tens of thousands of spectators outside Buckingham Palace, whose chants of 'We want Elizabeth! We want Philip!' turned to a roar of applause. Even after the pair had withdrawn from sight the crowd remained in good spirits, singing *All the Nice Girls Love a Sailor* throughout the afternoon in a tongue-in-cheek reference to the groom's military career.

A week later, American publication *Life* magazine was full of glowing praise for the occasion:

> In the ninth winter of Britain's austerity the skies cleared for a brief moment last week. Shining through came a fleeting, nostalgic glimpse of an ancient glory and a little pang of hope for better days to come.

The marriages celebrated by the royal House of Windsor in the first half of the twentieth century were a reflection of pride in time-honoured traditions, tinted with a spirit of innovation and romance. Not shy of revealing his fatherly emotion, after the ceremony of 1947 the king disclosed to the Archbishop: 'It is a far more moving thing to give your daughter away than to be married yourself.' The emphasis on royal family values that had underpinned Queen Victoria's popularity had culminated in grand, and thoroughly modern, celebrations of family occasions. Westminster Abbey, a stranger to wedding bells for centuries, quickly came into favour for the nuptials of prominent royals and allowed the public a much greater sense of participation. The nation's expectations, too, had changed. In a far cry from the restricted weddings enacted with little consideration of popular opinion, a journalist from the *Pathé Gazette* remarked of Princess Elizabeth: 'Mingled with her private happiness, is the sure knowledge that she must now enter a widening field of public duty and responsibility.'

The most fairytale of all royal weddings was, however, still to come. The latter half of the twentieth century witnessed technological advancements inviting the whole world to watch the ceremony, in its full colourful splendour. But the Archbishop of York's comment in 1947 that a royal marriage service was 'in all essentials the same as it would be for any cottagers who might be married in some country church' gained a new significance as it became apparent that the ceremony, however grand or modest, could not necessarily guarantee the harmony of a royal relationship.

Thousands swarm around the Victoria Memorial at the entrance of Buckingham Palace in the hope of cheering Princess Elizabeth and her husband. Chants of 'We want Elizabeth! We want Philip!' rang around Queen's Gardens until the couple appeared on the balcony.

THE MODERN
MARRIAGE

THE TWENTIETH CENTURY saw the royal wedding transformed into international spectacle; and a state celebration second only to a coronation. Just as the customs and traditions of royalty have evolved, the monarchy has adapted to modern values and ideas about what the institution of marriage represents. While the marriage of Queen Elizabeth and the Duke of Edinburgh boasts being the longest of any reigning British monarch, many of those closest to them have not enjoyed such matrimonial harmony. The idealised fairytale weddings providing such a source of comfort to a nation shattered by war came to earth with a bump as a string of royal marriages ended in divorce. As the more 'democratic' monarchy emerging from war grew to maturity, a more realistic perception of royal family life illustrated that even princes and princesses can suffer domestic misfortune.

The ceremonies themselves have differed greatly, in both character and media exposure. Until the 1980s, Westminster remained the favourite location. Between 1960 and 1986, Princess Anne, Princess Margaret, Princess Alexandra and Miss Sarah Ferguson all took the walk to the High Altar. In each case, the bridegroom looked back to admire his bride, having already entered inconspicuously by the south side door. Tradition dictates that having solemnised their vows, the couple sign the marital registers in the Chapel of St Edward the Confessor, gaining a brief respite from the glare of the cameras.

Although the wedding of Princess Margaret and photographer Anthony Armstrong-Jones was not officially a state occasion, the celebrations of 6 May 1960 roused a carnival atmosphere throughout London. Added to the glamour for which she was famous, her earlier renunciation of love in the name of royal protocol had stirred popular sympathies for the princess, which heightened when it transpired that she was to become the first member of the ruling family to wed an untitled husband. The proceedings commenced with her arrival at Westminster at 11.30 a.m., before a television audience of 20 million. The crowds lining the route heard the vows over loudspeakers. But, as expected, it was the bridal gown that stole the headlines. From the hand of royal favourite Norman Hartnell, it was a beautiful blend of

Opposite:
Before a crowd of thousands, the Prince and Princess of Wales stand on the balcony of Buckingham Palace after their grand wedding ceremony on 29 July 1981. Princess Diana smiles at her new husband as he kisses her hand.

Princess Margaret
and Antony
Armstrong-Jones
hold hands as they
leave Westminster
Abbey.

magnificence and simplicity. In an elegant cloud of white silk, the only jewels
she wore were a diamond rivière necklace bequeathed to her by her
grandmother Queen Mary, and a diamond tiara.

Following in the footsteps of her Aunt Margaret, Princess Anne made
the same vows, on the same spot, thirteen years later. On 14 November
1973, she married Captain Mark Phillips in a Tudor-style dress of white silk,
laced with pearls, silver thread and mirror jewels. Although it was estimated
that an audience of 50 million watched the televised ceremony, the couple
requested they should be allowed one concession to their privacy, and no
cameras faced them as they became man and wife.

The royal wedding was to reach the apotheosis of elegance and grandeur with the marriage of the Prince of Wales to the young and unassuming Lady Diana Spencer on 29 July 1981. Their engagement had been announced five months earlier, and in the interval things were much the same as *The Genius* had observed at the marriage of George III over two hundred years before: 'Scarce a paragraph of news, relating to any other matters, will go down.' Wedding gifts poured in, from the sapphire jewellery from the royal family of Saudi Arabia to a heart-shaped potato sent by a young child. Correspondingly, the public was deluged with an array of commemorative memorabilia, including specially issued stamps, tableware and coins. The ceremony itself was symbolic of the way in which Britain still clutched the idea of the royal fairytale wedding to its breast, and it did not prove a disappointment. The couple departed from recent tradition and chose a morning wedding at St Paul's Cathedral, ostensibly to allow for a larger guestlist. The news was not unwelcome, as it allowed for longer procession

On 8 June 1961, York Minster was the setting for the marriage of Edward, Duke of Kent and Katharine Worsley. This beautiful building had not played host to such an occasion since the nuptials of Edward III in 1328.

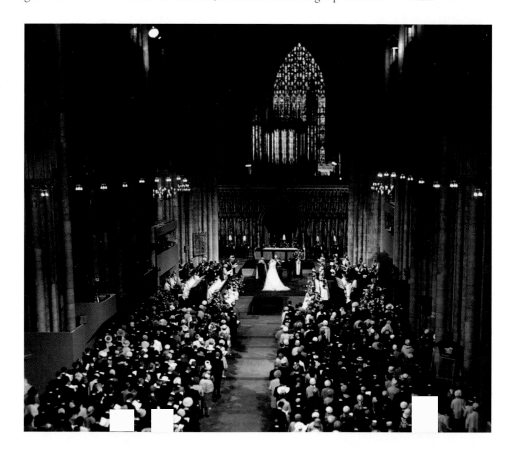

Above: Princess Anne continued the twentieth-century tradition for marrying in Westminster Abbey. She locks arms with new husband Mark Phillips, with brother Prince Edward in a Stuart kilt, and cousin Lady Sarah Armstrong-Jones.

Above, right: Official programmes of the wedding of Charles and Diana became a hugely popular piece of memorabilia.

routes of the royal family from Buckingham Palace, and the bride from Clarence House. As the crowds cheered loudly, and around 750 million viewers tuned in to the live broadcasts, Diana stepped out of the Glass Coach that had brought her to the steps of the Cathedral. Designers sat poised to take note of the cut of her dress, before scurrying off with their sketches; a replica was proudly displayed in the window of a West End shop before evening. It took several moments for her attendants to smooth out the ivory silk taffeta and antique lace skirt and its 25-foot train as it fluttered in the breeze, before a fanfare of trumpets announced that the bride had arrived. Escorted by her father, she eschewed normal custom and remained veiled even throughout the vows. Prince Charles wore the uniform of a commander of the Royal Navy.

Impressed with the scene before him, the Archbishop declared: 'This is the stuff of which fairytales are made.' Despite a couple of nervous slips during the vows, during which Diana muddled the order of the prince's names, the couple smiled their way through the ceremony. Demonstrating the modern values this couple had come to represent, Diana became the first royal bride to omit the word 'obey' from her vows. The acoustics of the cathedral complemented the refrain of Elgar's 'Pomp and Circumstance' as the procession made its way towards the carriages outside. As the couple enjoyed the wedding breakfast, where they were met with the sight of a 5-foot cake, the crowds grew impatient outside the palace. Just after 1pm, the chants turned to applause as the newlyweds stepped out on to the balcony and took their first public kiss as man and wife.

While the marriage of the heir to the throne perhaps demanded a display of love and lavishness in equal measure, the weddings of the queen's younger sons perhaps illustrate a greater sense of freedom. The nuptials of Prince Andrew and Sarah Ferguson on 23 July 1986 were in many ways a

Having solemnised their vows, Charles and Diana make the long walk from the altar to the royal carriage that awaits them outside the cathedral.

Prince Andrew and his bride Sarah Ferguson wave to the crowds as their open-top carriage departs Westminster and heads towards Buckingham Palace.

Although they opted for a relatively private service at St George's Chapel, Windsor, Prince Edward and bride Sophie Rhys Jones happily wave to their well-wishers. They married on 19 June 1999.

more traditional affair, and wedding bells came again to Westminster. But the pair brought a touch of their personalities to the occasion – the bridal gown was embroidered with beads forming the letter 'S', interwoven with hearts and anchors referring to her husband's military career. The new Duchess of York gave a thumbs-up to their well-wishers, and the couple teased the crowds from the palace balcony before giving them their public kiss.

The relationship of Prince Edward and Sophie Rhys-Jones had begun five years before their engagement was announced in 1999. In a move towards ceremonies that emphasised the wedding as a personal occasion rather than a matter of state, the two enjoyed a relatively private ceremony solemnised at St George's Chapel, Windsor Castle. It formed part of a rising trend for intimate weddings, preceded by the second marriage of Princess Anne to Timothy Laurence in 1992, and followed by Prince Charles' second marriage to Camilla Parker Bowles in a civil ceremony at Windsor in 2005.

CONCLUSION

A PUBLICATION CELEBRATING the tenth anniversary of Charles and Diana's wedding in 1991 gave voice to the revolution that had occurred in the popular view of royal weddings: 'Today, as far as the public is concerned, nothing less than a love match will do.' The statement not only demonstrates the dramatic shift in the perceived motivations for royal marriage, from dynastic stratagem to romantic ideal, but also the authority that the public seems to believe itself to wield in royal familial matters. In a far cry from the relative apathy and even ignorance of the medieval era, and as a direct result of the changes to royal protocol introduced in 1917, modern subjects seem to claim an entitlement to act as witnesses to the ceremony.

The history of the monarchy illustrates that the character and components of royal weddings can be as individual as the couple at the heart of the proceedings. The element of pomp and pageantry, the location, the dress, the music, the vows, the time of day – as the event approaches, all are subjected to considerations bound up in contemporary fashions, and balanced by wider ideological trends and personal preference. Nevertheless, glimpses of the monarchy's heritage continue to be expressed and honoured in the rituals and iconography of regal celebration, often most pertinently for those who hold the rights of a future heir to the throne. Selected from a rich and varied tapestry of tradition, from the sprig of myrtle to the relatively recent trend for a balcony appearance and public kiss, these elements are often seen to reflect the values of the couple themselves.

News of the forthcoming nuptials of Prince William and Kate Middleton has been eagerly embraced by a public somewhat starved of regal glamour and celebration in recent years. Having met outside of stately circles and enjoyed a long courtship, they represent a thoroughly modern royal match, and their lack of pretension has endeared them to the world. The occasion promises to be a vibrant blend of tradition and modern taste, and is set to rekindle the national spirit of optimism that always attends the wedding of a well-liked royal. As *The Times* articulated in 1858:

A wedding brings out all that is genial in the nature of those who come within its influence. How much more is this the case when the pair to be wedded are of Royal blood, young, and attached to each other.

As with the popular matches of Arthur and Catherine, Victoria and Albert, and Charles and Diana before them, no matter what the face of the occasion proves to be, this tide of sentiment will provide the backdrop for what could herald a new era for the British royal wedding.

Prince William and Kate Middleton announced their engagement on 16 November 2010, and it was met with an outpouring of public excitement. It was later announced that the marriage would take place on 29 April 2011 in Wesminster Abbey.

PLACES TO VISIT

Visitors are advised to check opening times before visiting.

The Banqueting House, Whitehall, London SW1 2ER.
Telephone: 020 3166 6154. Website: www.hrp.org.uk/banquetinghouse

Discover Greenwich Centre, Old Royal Naval College, Greenwich SE10 9LW.
Telephone: 020 8269 4747.
Website: www.oldroyalnavalcollege.org/discover-greenwich

Fashion Museum, Assembly Rooms, Bennett Street, Bath BA1 2QH.
Telephone: 01225 477789. Website: www.museumodcostume.co.uk

Kensington Palace, State Apartments, Kensington Gardens, London W8 4PX.
Telephone: 0844 482 7777. Website: www.hrp.org.uk/kensingtonpalace

Kew Palace, Royal Botanic Gardens, Richmond, Surrey TW9 3AB
Telephone: 0844 482 7777. Website: www.hrp.org.uk/kewpalace

The Queen's Gallery, Buckingham Palace, Birdcage Walk, London SW1A 1AA.
Telephone: 020 7766 7301. Website: www.royalcollection.org.uk

St James's Park, London SW1.
Telephone: 020 7930 1793. Website: www.royalparks.org.uk

St Paul's Cathedral, St Paul's Churchyard, London EC4M 8AD.
Telephone: 020 7246 8350. Website: www.stpauls.co.uk

Westminster Abbey, 20 Deans Yard, London SW1P 3PA.
Telephone: 020 7222 5152. Website: www.westminster-abbey.org

Winchester Cathedral, 1 The Close, Winchester, Hampshire S023 9LS.
Telephone: 01962 857200. Website: www.winchester-cathedral.org.uk

Windsor Castle, Windsor SL4 1NJ.
Telephone: 020 7930 9625. Website: www.royalcollection.org.uk

York Minster, York YO1 7HH.
Telephone: 0844 939 0011. Website: www.yorkminster.org

This map shows the procession route of the royal carriages to and from St Paul's Cathedral for the wedding of Prince Charles and Diana Spencer in 1981.

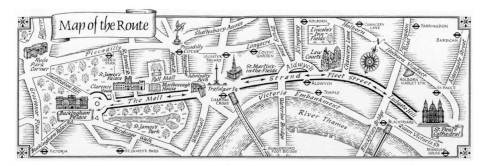

INDEX